Table of

Sponsor: One who binds himself to answer for another; one who is responsible for another's default.

"THE YEAR OF EQUIPPING" WITHIN THE CELL GROUP

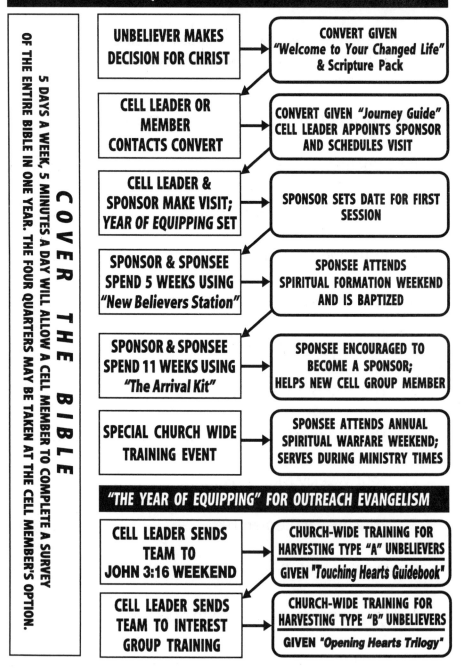

COVER THE BIBLE

OF THE ENTIRE BIBLE IN ONE YEAR. THE FOUR QUARTERS MAY BE TAKEN AT THE CELL MEMBER'S OPTION.

5 DAYS A WEEK, 5 MINUTES A DAY WILL ALLOW A CELL MEMBER TO COMPLETE A SURVEY

UNBELIEVER MAKES DECISION FOR CHRIST → CONVERT GIVEN *"Welcome to Your Changed Life"* & Scripture Pack

CELL LEADER OR MEMBER CONTACTS CONVERT → CONVERT GIVEN *"Journey Guide"* CELL LEADER APPOINTS SPONSOR AND SCHEDULES VISIT

CELL LEADER & SPONSOR MAKE VISIT; YEAR OF EQUIPPING SET → SPONSOR SETS DATE FOR FIRST SESSION

SPONSOR & SPONSEE SPEND 5 WEEKS USING *"New Believers Station"* → SPONSEE ATTENDS SPIRITUAL FORMATION WEEKEND AND IS BAPTIZED

SPONSOR & SPONSEE SPEND 11 WEEKS USING *"The Arrival Kit"* → SPONSEE ENCOURAGED TO BECOME A SPONSOR; HELPS NEW CELL GROUP MEMBER

SPECIAL CHURCH WIDE TRAINING EVENT → SPONSEE ATTENDS ANNUAL SPIRITUAL WARFARE WEEKEND; SERVES DURING MINISTRY TIMES

"THE YEAR OF EQUIPPING" FOR OUTREACH EVANGELISM

CELL LEADER SENDS TEAM TO JOHN 3:16 WEEKEND → CHURCH-WIDE TRAINING FOR HARVESTING TYPE "A" UNBELIEVERS GIVEN *"Touching Hearts Guidebook"*

CELL LEADER SENDS TEAM TO INTEREST GROUP TRAINING → CHURCH-WIDE TRAINING FOR HARVESTING TYPE "B" UNBELIEVERS GIVEN *"Opening Hearts Trilogy"*

Introduction

Every new member in your Cell Group needs a Sponsor. Your Cell Leader will prayerfully select a Sponsor for him or her. If you are approached to undertake that ministry, this book will be very valuable to you. Read it carefully, praying for insights that will deepen your own walk with the Lord through helping another person. Use it as a reference book during the weeks you sponsor.

This book will help you whether your Sponsee is someone you already know or someone you are now meeting for the first time.

If your Sponsee is a new believer, *The New Believers Station* materials should be used for the first five weeks of your time together. A separate booklet, the *New Believers Station Sponsor's Guide,* should be used for these sessions.

If your Sponsee is not a new believer, you begin your Sponsor-Sponsee relationship by sharing *The Arrival Kit.* A *Weekly Sponsor's Guide* is included in the back of it to help you.

The Sponsor-Sponsee relationship does not last forever. After three or four months, your relationship will change. You will minister together as *Partners,* sharing your faith with unbelievers as you take the *Touching Hearts Guidebook* training. At that time, you will also help your Sponsee become a Sponsor of another incoming person in your Cell Group. May God anoint you for this new stage of ministry as you begin to nurture another Christian!

Use this book as a guide as you serve as a Sponsor for the first time.

Use the *New Believers Station Sponsor's Guide* when sponsoring a new believer.

Use the *Weekly Sponsor's Guide* when sponsoring a person studying *The Arrival Kit.*

You will then become a Partner with your Sponsee as you begin to reach "Type A" unbelievers.

5

From him the whole body, joined and held together by EVERY SUPPORTING LIGAMENT, *grows and builds itself up in love, as each part does its work. (Ephesians 4:16)*

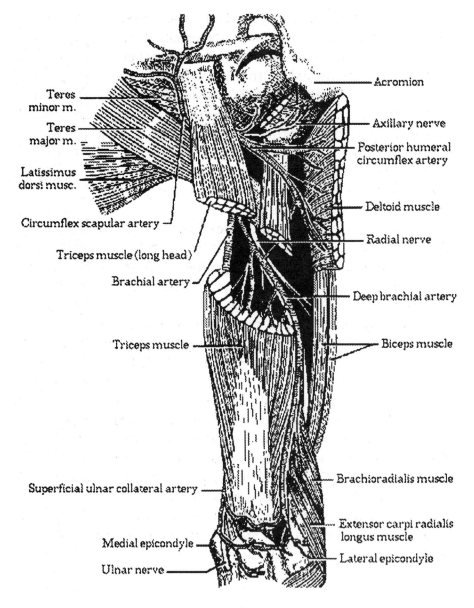

6

1 The Sponsor's Lifestyle

Thoughtfully read this Scripture passage. As you do, find yourself in it. Where are you described?

> It was he who gave some to be apostles, some to be prophets, some to be evangelists, and some to be pastors and teachers, to prepare God's people for works of service, so that the body of Christ may be built up until we all reach unity in the faith and in the knowledge of the Son of God and become mature, attaining to the whole measure of the fullness of Christ. Then we will no longer be infants, tossed back and forth by the waves, and blown here and there by every wind of teaching and by the cunning and craftiness of men in their deceitful scheming. Instead, speaking the truth in love, we will in all things grow up into him who is the Head, that is, Christ. From him the whole body, joined and held together by every supporting ligament, grows and builds itself up in love, as each part does its work. (Ephesians 4:11-16)

Here are some of the categories mentioned. Which of them would you place yourself in at this moment?

1. Mature servants, called "apostles," "prophets," "evangelists," "pastors," and "teachers."
2. Mature Christians who have entered into the "fullness of Christ."
3. Infants who are blown around by every wind of teaching.

You probably placed yourself somewhere between the second and the third categories. You're not exactly an infant, but you would also not say you are a mature Christian. There is a fourth category in this scripture passage that should precisely define your present condition. Underline it in your own Bible so you will remember it:

From him the whole body, joined and held together by every supporting ligament, grows and builds itself up in love, as each part does its work.

Sometimes we tend to think of "full-time Christian workers" as the *ministers*, but that's not what Ephesians 4:11-16 says. Those who are most mature are to become the servants of the Body of Christ. The members of that body are to be *supporting ligaments.*

The New Webster's Dictionary of the English Language defines "ligament" as:

A band of strong fibrous tissue connecting bones at a joint, or serving to hold in place and support body organs. What ties or unites one thing or part to another; a bond.

YOU ARE A SUPPORTING LIGAMENT

For centuries, the Body of Christ has suffered from ignoring Paul's teaching in this passage. The church has been like the "dry bones" Ezekiel saw in chapter 37:1-6:

The hand of the LORD was upon me, and he brought me out by the Spirit of the LORD and set me in the middle of a valley; it was full of bones. He led me back and forth among them, and I saw a great many bones on the floor of the valley, bones that were very dry. He asked me, "Son of man, can these bones live?" I said, "O Sovereign LORD, you alone know." Then he said to me, "Prophesy to these bones and say to them, 'Dry bones, hear the word of the LORD! This is what the Sovereign LORD says to these bones: I will make breath enter you, and you will come to life. I will attach tendons [ligaments] to you and make flesh come upon you and cover you with skin; I will put breath in you, and you will come to life. Then you will know that I am the LORD.'"

8

We have placed a great deal of stress on the importance of the mature parts of the body, the "five fold ministries," but we have failed to see that for every pastor, teacher, evangelist, prophet or apostle, there are literally scores and scores of believers who have never been equipped to serve as *ligaments*. The Body of Christ requires *each part to do its work*.

You may not be an *apostle*, but you are certainly a *ligament*. You can tie or unite yourself to another Cell member, and create a bond of love. You can support another believer— right now!

That's what it means to be a Sponsor! This is not some tricky word which has been coined to provide extra work for you to do as a Cell Group member. It is the very first step you can take to become a supporting ligament in Christ's Body.

—A TRUE STORY—

Max is a wonderful Christian who was serving his Lord at the highest levels when we first met. I noticed he walked with a limp. When he wanted to stand up and talk to me he would always lean against a wall or hold my arm. Tactfully I said, "Max, what's the problem with your leg?" He replied, "Ralph, some years ago a disease attacked my leg and destroyed the ligaments around the ankle. The bones are fine, but all support for my ankle bones is gone. The ligaments don't give me any support. I used to love to run; now I can only limp."

In your Cell Group, is there a "Max" who limps because a "supporting ligament" has never been provided? Perhaps you, yourself, are reading this sentence and saying, "I am like that. I limp along in my Christian life today because no one took the time to support me when I first became a believer." If so, you are learning why it is so important to be a ligament in your Cell Group. There are two problems when ligaments do not function properly. The first is that a bone is not supported; the second is that the ligament itself is weak, diseased, and useless.

9

We will use a special word for ligaments in this book. We will call them "Sponsors." This is how Webster (op. cit.) defines the term:

One who binds himself to answer for another; one who is responsible for another's default . . .

SPONSORING IS YOUR
FIRST MINISTRY IN A CELL GROUP

A newborn baby is totally consumed with his own needs. He cries when he is wet and when he is hungry. He offers no support for anyone in the family. This is one of the characteristics of being a child.

I recall when my first grandchild was born. Nathan kept his parents hopping to meet his needs. A couple of years later, baby Ruth entered the home. Immediately Nathan wanted to help her. We snapped a photo of him, not yet three, proudly holding her in his little lap and feeding her with a bottle.

It's interesting to see how quickly a child grows out of the first stage into the second one. Parents may think, "This child is too young to feed the baby!" Nevertheless, the child needs to be trusted to do so. It is through such activities that further maturity will take place in his life.

Are you mature enough to hold a spiritual bottle and feed another member of your Cell Group? Of course you are! And the act of doing so is vital to your own development.

SPONSORING IS VITAL TO YOUR OWN GROWTH

Someone has said, "You will be the same person you are now five years from today, except for the people you meet and the books you read." Of the two alternatives, meeting new people will have the more profound effect on your life. Attaching yourself to a Sponsee will sensitize you to the Lord's voice. Through the experiences of meeting together, you will see things within your own life that will cause significant

10

changes in you. Exploring together with your Sponsee will cause you to grow significantly.

SPONSORING IS VITAL TO CELL LIFE

Unless all the ligaments function together, your Cell Group will become dry bones. It will become inflexible in outlook or habits and it will die. The very heart of a "Basic Christian Community," another term for a Cell Group, is for its members to become responsible to, and for, one another. That important ingredient is what makes a Cell Group grow.

WHAT TO DO IF YOUR SPONSEE IS NOT TOO RESPONSIVE

Living in the Kingdom of God must be generated by the Holy Spirit stirring within the believer's spirit. The very first thing to learn is whether your Sponsee has *truly* accepted Christ as Savior and Lord. You cannot expect a spiritual corpse to show signs of life. Being "dead *in* sin" is one reason a person who claims to be a Christian isn't responsive. Check it out.

But being "alive *to* sin" can also be a problem causing a lack of responsiveness. Scripture tells us the believer can *grieve, resist, quench,* or *be filled* with the Holy Spirit (see Acts 7:51; Ephesians 4:30-32; 1 Thessalonians 5:19; Ephesians 5:18). Is your Sponsee *grieving, resisting,* or *quenching* the Spirit? After Adam and Eve sinned, they avoided God. Check this out, too!

If your Sponsee is not responsive, the first thing is to establish a personal bond to provide deep sharing between the two of you. Confession of sin and awareness of strongholds is the first step in breaking the bondage of Satan. There is no timetable for this to take place. Patience and prayer are your tools of warfare for your Sponsee. Don't set conditions on how far you are willing to go before you drop the relationship! In addition, if your Sponsee is not responsive, share your problem with your Cell Leader.

2   **Jesus and His Cell Group**

Jesus formed a Cell Group when He began His public ministry. In the Godhead, He had lived forever in community with the Father and the Holy Spirit. He knew the importance of dwelling in relationships. Even before He performed His first miracle at Cana, He had formed a special Cell Group of men who would be with Him for the rest of His time on earth.

Jesus is the classic example of a Cell Leader. After relating to many persons, He selected those who would comprise His Cell Group. In Mark 3:14, we are told He did so *"that they might be with him."* That is the value of a Cell Group: people form relationships as they meet together with one another. This does not occur when people meet as a "congregation" of forty or fifty persons. It is difficult to attain transparency and edification when the group is larger than fifteen persons. It can only take place in a Cell Group.

Jesus modelled the life of a Cell Leader. The study of the way He ministered on a one-to-one basis to His disciples provides principles you can apply in your ministry as a Sponsor to another person.

The times these twelve men spent with Jesus were as important to their spiritual development as His teachings. All the words of Jesus recorded in the Gospels can be read aloud in less than an hour, but He spent at least three years interacting with them.

Jesus' ministry in the Cell Group had four powerful impacts on each member:

12

1. The group was impacted through His *modelling*.

Jesus spent much time modelling the lifestyle of how a person should live in the Kingdom of God. His nights spent in prayer, the journeys they took together, the way He showed them the power of God—all these demonstrated Kingdom values which could not be communicated through lectures. Observation provided a greater impact than instruction. A Sponsor knows that time spent together with the Sponsee is important.

2. The group was impacted by *mutual sharing*.

Jesus' Cell Group not only observed *Him*; they also observed *each other*. Simultaneously, they saw the way *He* lived, and contrasted it with the behaviour of the *others* in the group. Peter's brashness, James' desire for status, Thomas' cynicism and John's tender heart were all revealed alongside Jesus' character. Conflicts between the men were exposed, and caused Jesus to minister to them separately as would a Sponsor. (See Mark 10:35-38, 41-45; Luke 22:31-34.)

A Sponsor must be aware that the members of the Cell Group will make an impact on the Sponsee. Observations of the Sponsee's reaction to other Cell Group members may reveal areas of inner conflict where ministry should be provided in private sessions. This interaction may be very significant in some cases.

—A TRUE STORY—

Doug was a new believer we had worked with for many months prior to his surrender to Christ. We sensed an inner anger but its source was hidden. We included him in our Cell Group and he seemed comfortable in the group. An old man visited us. He had a sharp, raspy voice and was dominant. Doug became very upset. When we met as Sponsor-Sponsee that week I said, "Doug, you were angry at that old man without good reason. You have never seen him before. What's going on inside you?"

Doug then poured out the pain caused by his own father, who had the same sharp, raspy voice when he spoke as the old man in our group. His father had made him work for years in the family business, promising that one day Doug would inherit the ownership of the company. Suddenly, his father sold the business to a stranger and retired. When Doug faced him with his betrayal, his father shrugged his shoulders and said, "Tough luck!" Doug moved miles away from his father and had lived with seething hate toward him for five years. It was in the context of our Cell Group that his problem was uncovered. We spent many hours in our Sponsor-Sponsee times working through his pain.

3. The group was impacted by teachable moments.
Do you remember this event from Matthew 17:14-20?

When they came to the crowd, a man approached Jesus and knelt before him. "Lord, have mercy on my son," he said. "He has seizures and is suffering greatly. He often falls into the fire or into the water. I brought him to your disciples, but they could not heal him." "O unbelieving and perverse generation," Jesus replied, "how long shall I stay with you? How long shall I put up with you? Bring the boy here to me." Jesus rebuked the demon, and it came out of the boy, and he was healed from that moment. Then the disciples came to Jesus in private and asked, "Why couldn't we drive it out?" He replied, "Because you have so little faith. I tell you the truth, if you have faith as small as a mustard seed, you can say to this mountain, 'Move from here to there' and it will move. Nothing will be impossible for you."

In this event, the twelve Cell Group members were embarrassed by their impotence in ministering to others. Jesus waited for that moment to explain an important truth. They needed to learn that some needs would only be met by prayer and fasting.

In the life of a Sponsor, there will be "teachable moments" that cannot be anticipated. Teachable moments are those specific times when the Sponsee is ready for assistance. "Ligaments" must be sensitive to special circumstances. A Sponsor should learn to make good use of these unexpected turns of events which provide "teachable moments."

4. The group was impacted by mutual learning from one another. Note this event, recorded in Matthew 16:13-17:

> When Jesus came to the region of Caesarea Philippi, he asked his disciples, "Who do people say the Son of Man is?" They replied, "Some say John the Baptist; others say Elijah; and still others, Jeremiah or one of the prophets." "But what about you?" he asked. "Who do you say I am?" Simon Peter answered, "You are the Christ, the Son of the living God." Jesus replied, "Blessed are you, Simon son of Jonah, for this was not revealed to you by man, but by my Father in heaven . . ."

Notice the strategy of our Lord in this event. He first asked a question to steer their thinking in a certain direction: *"Who do people say the Son of Man is?"* He is not really interested in their answers. He immediately asks another question: *"Who do you say I am?"* Peter's reply was immediately affirmed by Jesus.

But the question we might ask ourselves is, "Why did He use this devious method to draw that statement out of the group? He could have simply said, *'I am the Christ, the Son of the Living God.'"*

That was not what He wanted. His desire was to let the disciples learn from one another. There is great value in drawing out a thought rather than teaching it. The fact that one of their peers stated this great truth had a profound impact on the group.

You may find this tool of Jesus to be helpful as you minister to your Sponsee. For example, a man had just entered our Cell Group and it was my assignment to be his Sponsor. As we shared, he admitted he had gambled away all his savings. Rather than lecturing him about this addiction, I waited until our next Cell meeting. I asked the group, "Have any of you overcome the temptation to make a killing through betting or card playing?" Those who shared their own stories or their experiences with family members who gambled made a great impact on my friend. In our next session together, he spoke openly of their answers and what he learned from them.

Jesus has given us many other insights into the way to shape values in the lives of others. As you read the four Gospels, think about what He said and the way He went about His ministry to His Cell Group members. He is the Master, and thus the master example of how to build up others.

3 Sponsoring and Accountability

*. . . I will show my love to the one I called 'Not my loved one.'
I will say to those called 'Not my people,' 'You are my people';
and they will say, 'You are my God.'" (Hosea 2:23)*

Let's review the definition of a Sponsor:

One who binds himself to answer for another; one who is responsible for another's default . . .

Contrast this definition with the attitude of the murderer Cain when God asked him in Genesis 4:9:

"Where is your brother Abel?"
"I don't know," he replied. "Am I my brother's keeper?"

These two thoughts contrast the life we are to live in Christ and the life which is lived under Satan's control. Sponsoring is not simply getting together once a week to have a meeting. It is a "bonding" process. Living the Christian life is becoming responsible for someone you would otherwise ignore. *I am my brother's keeper!* I enter into this relationship with another person ready to be accountable for what I do and how I respond to what he or she does. In this tie, the Sponsee must be accountable to you for what you are doing to provide an atmosphere for his or her spiritual growth. There must be mutual accountability and responsibility.

The little tasks you do together will reveal the depth of accountability the two of you have for one another. One of these tasks is the weekly review of Scriptures to be memorized. Lazy minds will avoid this discipline. Nevertheless, if the two of you agree that Scripture memorization is a worthwhile task, there should be no excuse for not reviewing Scripture memory verses in your weekly meetings. Another example is being on time for your get-togethers instead of chronically showing up late. This is another "little sign" of responsible behaviour. Caring for one another is a two-way process. The best ability is dependability.

A CLASSIC EXAMPLE OF BEING RESPONSIBLE

Jean Vanier took a doctorate in philosophy. He could easily have buried himself in a university as a lecturer. However, his walk with Christ called him into a different path. He founded *l'Arche* in Trosly-Breuil in the suburban area of Paris and lived for 14 years in a house with people who were mentally handicapped. He found that those who felt excluded, worthless and unloved were radically changed by their experiences with him.

For Vanier, it would have been a simple matter to abandon the first two men he brought from an asylum to begin *l'Arche*. He rejected this temptation, knowing that what they needed was patient acceptance. His responsible care caused significant changes in their personalities.

Your entry into the Sponsor's ministry is an important step in learning how to live as an authentic Christian. Instead of saying, "The Cell Group for Myself," you are saying, "Myself for the Community." Launching your first ministry to a Sponsee may be the first important step you take toward becoming a mature, responsible believer. Philippians 2:3-4 teaches us:

Do nothing out of selfish ambition or vain conceit, but in humility consider others better than yourselves. Each of you should look not only to your own interests, but also to the interests of others.

Sponsoring is much, much more than simply becoming "prayer partners." That term simply does not embrace or clinch what needs to happen. We must do more than "pray for one another." We must love someone else so much we are willing to be responsible for this person. It takes time to move from our self-protecting egoism to this lifestyle of true love.

BEING RESPONSIBLE MEANS MAKING SACRIFICES

I was called to be a witness in an ugly divorce settlement. Before pronouncing his verdict, the wise judge said to the estranged couple, "I have listened for years to reports of marriages that break down. This is my conclusion: Love is caring enough for someone else so much you will make great sacrifices for that person. You have never cared for each other at that level. It is the reason your marriage has been destroyed."

Do not enter into the relationship with your Sponsee lightly. Love means making great sacrifices for him or her. It means answering the calls of inner pain. It means rejoicing when breakthroughs come. It means longing for more light to be within your friend—and yourself—as you grow together in Christ.

EXAMPLE: THE BLOOD COVENANT OF THE OLD TESTAMENT

In 1 Samuel 20, Saul is seeking to destroy David. Jonathan, Saul's son, enters into a special covenant with him. It is mentioned in verse 16:

> So Jonathan made a covenant with the house of David, saying, "May the LORD call David's enemies to account."

When Saul threatened to have David murdered, this covenant between the two men saved David's life. Describing this, Scripture explains in 1 Samuel 20:17:

> And Jonathan had David reaffirm his oath out of love for him, because he loved him as he loved himself.

The covenant between these two men is an example of the total commitment that will begin to grow between you and your

19

Sponsee. Relating to the Sponsee must be a priority in your life. Out of that priority, a two-way pattern of being responsible for, and accountable to, each other will develop.

BEING RESPONSIBLE
DOESN'T MEAN BECOMING A CRUTCH

A Chinese proverb says, "Every tub must stand on its own bottom." In a later chapter, we will discuss the importance of not becoming a problem-solver or a "rescuer" for your Sponsee. False friends are those who only see good qualities and ignore areas of great need. A characteristic of a false Sponsor is one who does not help his Sponsee stand on his own two feet.

Being accountable for your Sponsee does not include becoming responsible for making decisions for him or her. That is not healthy! Instead, walk together through each problem, pointing out conditions which may not be obvious to the Sponsee.

STAGES IN AN ACCOUNTABILITY RELATIONSHIP

Accountability takes time! We must earn the right to hear the deep things in the heart of another person. Transparency in your relationship will gradually reveal needs that are far too personal to share in the beginning stages. Love and respect will develop as you get to know each other better. As common interests are discovered, they will create powerful sharing times which will bond you together. Expect to move through these four stages as you minister to your Sponsee:

1. Get-Acquainted Stage.
When we first meet someone we do not know, we associate this stranger with people we know who have similar features. The association may be to tone of voice, facial characteristics, etc. (The tone of voice was the issue which triggered Marvin's reaction to the old man.) Thus, if a person resembles someone I love, I will respond positively. If the similarity is to someone who has hurt me in the past, I will be very defensive in my responses.

Being responsible for, and accountable to, each other is not possible in this first stage. Therefore, your first meetings together should focus on getting acquainted, using nonthreatening questions. For many years, these four questions have been used to help deepen relationships in this first stage:

- Where did you live between the ages of 7 and 12?
- What form of transportation did your family use?
- Whom were you emotionally closest to during that time?
- When did the word "God" first become meaningful to you?

2. Conflict Stage.

Once you get to know each other, there may be conflicts which surface out of your lifestyles, value systems, or priorities. Sometimes this conflict is severe and sometimes it is very mild. At this stage, the two of you must learn to accept one another and agree that your differences will not sever your relationship. Ask your Cell Leader for help if you cannot work through this by yourself.

3. Community Stage.

In this third stage, which should be reached within a few sessions together, you will enter the time when accountability can take place. You will have earned each other's respect. Now is the time when real needs can be surfaced and steps taken to bring Christ's Lordship into focus.

4. Ministry and Outreach Stage.

Finally, you will enter into a relationship of deep trust. As you see breakthroughs in the needs of the Sponsee, change the focus of your get-togethers to helping others. Do not let your relationship become enclosed and insular! (Remember Nathan, who wanted to hold the bottle to feed Ruthie.)

4 Six Things a Sponsor Does

A SPONSOR LISTENS

We were taught to read and write in school, but most people have had no formal training in listening. If we never learn how to listen, we will never really understand deeply the frame of reference of another person's lifestyle.

Listening means we get inside another person's way of seeing the world. Once we do this, we see the world the way he or she sees the world, and we understand how he or she feels.

Look at this illustration:

Actually, these two persons are not talking to each other. They are talking to themselves! It's easy to project our beliefs and values onto another person, distorting what that individual knows and values. To minister to your Sponsee, you must guard against assuming your beliefs automatically make sense.

1. Avoid these four errors in listening:
   1. IGNORING WHAT IS BEING SAID, as you think, "What am I going to say in response to this?"

   2. PRETENDING TO LISTEN, as you turn off the conversation with comments like "Yes. Uh-huh. Right . . . "

   3. SELECTIVE LISTENING, choosing only what you want to hear and discarding the rest of the comments.

   4. ATTENTIVE LISTENING, paying attention to what is being said but not sensing the feelings behind the words.

2. Use "Deliberative Listening."

At this level, you will seek to understand the needs, fears, joys, and strong convictions of the Sponsee. This is sometimes called "active listening." It is powerful because it gives you an understanding of spiritual needs and awarenesses. Instead of assuming thoughts and feelings, you're dealing with the reality inside another person's head and heart. You are *listening to understand.*

Remember that *satisfied* needs do not open a person to grow in Christ. Only the *unsatisfied* needs do that. When you really listen, your Sponsee will share with you the depths of his or her life.

3. Listen with Acceptance.

A man who was struggling to be free of drugs said to me, "When I have told Christians of my fight to keep away from drugs, they have avoided me after that. They seem to be very accepting of the person who tells how they *had* been using drugs, but they don't want contact with someone *still* on them!"

It would be a terrible thing for your Sponsee to sense that kind of an attitude in you as you listen to his or her heart-felt needs. Listen with acceptance, not judging what you are hearing and registering condemnation.

4. How the Sponsee will react to the way you listen:

It is important to pay attention to your body language as you listen. Studies have shown that 55% of the impact you are making as you listen comes from your non-verbal cues—the way you sit, what you do with your arms, hands, and eyes etc. Thirty-eight per cent of your influence will be reflected by your vocal expression, and only 7% by the words you say!

For example, look at this illustration. Would you say this listener is speaking volumes without even opening his mouth?

Listening is hard work—particularly when you are seeking to hear what the Sponsee is saying with your *physical* ears and what the Lord is saying to you about the matter with your *spiritual* ears.

A SPONSOR INTERCEDES

The reason it is important to listen is that you can take your Sponsee's sharing to the Lord in *intercession.* Intercession is approaching the Lord on behalf of another person. The word comes from two Latin words meaning "to go between." Being a Sponsor to another person involves pleading with God for mercy for your Sponsee, who is in need. It does not mean you seek to manipulate God to do something you think would solve a problem. Instead, your intercession can determine whether God's grace is brought into certain situations or whether Satan's power will continue to control that area.

1. Examples of Intercession:

The passage in Genesis 18:1-2 and 18:16-33 tells of the impending destruction of Sodom and Gomorrah and Abraham's intercession for it. God responded to his pleas. In Exodus 32:1–14, the intercession of Moses spared Israel from

God's judgment. In Acts 12:1-19, Peter was delivered from prison through the intercession of the house church.

2. Intercession for your Sponsee brings life.

In 1 John 5:16, there are special situations which you will undoubtedly face in your ministry as a Sponsor. John the Elder explains that there are two types of sin. One of them is called a *"sin that leads to death."* Many expositors point out that the "death" referred to here can either be spiritual or physical (see 1 Corinthians 11:29-30). But John goes on to speak about *"a sin that does not lead to death."* Someone has called this "stupid sinning"—the things that an immature Christian does out of ignorance, repeating old habits rooted before coming to Christ.

For example, one Sponsor became close enough to his Sponsee to know he had a habit of secretly smoking. The fact that he hid his habit revealed he knew it was not a good thing to be doing. What should the Sponsor do? The relationship between them was not yet strong enough for him to confront the hypocrisy and the habit. In this case, the Sponsor obeyed the instructions concerning intercession in 1 John 5:16:

> If anyone sees his brother commit a sin that does not lead to death, he should pray and God will give him life.

The Sponsor took the situation to the Lord in intercessory prayer. As he did so, a great peace flooded his soul. It was as though the Lord had said, "Leave this situation to me. I will deal with it."

In fact, that is *exactly* what the Greek verbs indicate should happen in such a situation. The passage in the NASB version reads, *"he should ask and God will for him give life to those who commit sin not leading to death."* The passage is saying, "If you pray for your weaker brother, who is involved in stupid sinning which does not lead to death as a punishment, then God will give you—the intercessor—as well as your Sponsee life!

25

Thus, there are situations you will face in ministry to the Sponsee where you simply present the situation to the Lord and then rest in the knowledge He will deal with it.

—A TRUE STORY—

My Grandfather Zimmerman was the most spiritual man I knew in my boyhood days. His son, Roy, my uncle, lived a wild life and totally ignored the love and concern of his father. When I was ten years old, I was shocked to learn of some of Uncle Roy's escapades. I said, "Paw Paw, why don't you disinherit him? He doesn't deserve to have your last name!" With a wink and a crinkled smile, he said to me, "Let's leave him to Papa." (He always called the Heavenly Father "Papa," his equivalent expression for "Abba.") He taught me the importance of intercession and trust in the Father to deal with circumstances. Both of these men are now with the Lord, but before Uncle Roy grew old he made a paradigm shift to become a spiritual man. Paw Paw never lived to see it—but he knew in God's timing his son's heart would turn to the Lord!

The Greek word used for the Holy Spirit is *parakletos*. It literally means, "One called alongside to help." That same word is used as a participle to describe the spiritual gift of encouraging in Romans 12:8. That gift will be operating in you as you serve as a Sponsor, for you will literally be fulfilling the calling to be "one called alongside to help!" The empowerment of God upon your life will be present as you intercede in prayer. Expect it—experience it—and know that if you had never reached out to minister as a Sponsor, you might never know the impact of intercession.

In Romans 8:26 we are told:

. . . the Spirit helps us in our weakness. We do not know what we ought to pray for, but the Spirit himself intercedes for us with groans that words cannot express.

26

fellow pilgrim who is also on the journey. Your influence will come from letting Christ be revealed in you.

A SPONSOR TEACHES

There are two things we usually visualize when the idea of *teaching* is mentioned. The first is a classroom, and the second is a blackboard! Inserted into this picture is a teacher who explains facts not yet learned by a student. If that is your impression of what you are to do as a Sponsor, take an eraser and rub out those impressions from the blackboard of your mind.

What you will do as a "teacher" must be based on a more biblical model. In Jesus' day, the instruction method was essentially oral, with a strong emphasis on memorization. The goal was not to collect *information,* but to cause a *transformation* in the life of the learner. Life-sharing companionship marked the relationship; the student was constantly with his teacher. Furthermore, the disciple was expected to assume the role of a servant to his teacher, performing menial tasks like carrying loads, buying food, scrubbing floors, etc.

Thus, the imparting of information took place in the context of a continual relationship. How can that be duplicated in the relationship between you and your Sponsee?

First of all, the information you are to share is provided for you during your times together. The *New Believers Station* and *The Arrival Kit* provide the contents for your weekly sessions. It is important that you yourself have completed each unit before you meet with your Sponsee. It is important for you to review the weekly material you have already completed. As you do so, think about truths which need to be particularly emphasized. Think of personal illustrations from your own life history that might facilitate the discussion.

There will be many topics you may need to talk about which are not covered by the written materials. These may include an explanation of spiritual gifts observed by the Sponsee in the Cell Group, the importance of true worship during praise times, etc. New believers are often gullible and open to cult

29

teachings, not understanding there are "wolves" within religious circles. Like a good shepherd, protect your lamb from these scavengers.

A SPONSOR SETS THE PACE

Pacesetting is a term borrowed from running. It describes one who sets the pace for others to follow. It is "leading the way," showing the direction to be taken. The pacesetter shows how to run with steadiness instead of spurts. The inexperienced runner may go too fast and burn out before the race is over, or jog too slowly and finish last.

There are many areas of Christian growth that require pacesetting. Spending an hour together in prayer is one example. Probably no one has entered into such a lengthy time of prayer until someone has led the way to do it. Witnessing to the lost is another area which always requires a pacesetter to lead out in visitation and cultivation.

—A TRUE STORY—

In the prime years of his career, Gil Dodds became the fastest man in the world when running a mile race. This world-record holder worked as a track coach at Wheaton College. As a freshman, I joined the track team without any previous experience. I did so simply because of my admiration for this famous man. The first day of practice, I was ordered to run a mile as fast as I could while the stopwatch clocked my speed. Desiring to impress Gil, I poured myself into the first three laps. With one more lap to go, I was out of breath, strength, and desire to take another step. With sweat stinging my half-closed eyes, I was about to drop out. It was at this point that Gil appeared at my side. Quietly he said, "Ralph, watch my pace. Just keep moving your feet to stay with me." I shall never forget the thrill that went through me as I watched his shoes touch the track and provide a pace for me. I didn't break any

30

records that day (or any other day), but God showed me in a personal way the difference a pacesetter can make.

A SPONSOR INVOLVES THE SPONSEE WITH OTHER CHRISTIANS

Do not allow the relationship you have with your Sponsee to become exclusive! Seek to develop contacts with others who have had similar experiences. Expand the relationships of the Sponsee with other members of the Cell Group and others in the Zone. Recognize that these new relationships will supplement and undergird your own mentoring.

If you do not do this, you may end up with an "echo" of yourself as a result of your sponsoring. *Echoes are never voices!* Dominating the Sponsee or limiting contacts with others in the Cell Group is very unwise.

I came to know a very gifted pastor who launched an experimental church next to a seminary campus. His desire was to inspire young men as they prepared for Christian service, and he captured the hearts and admiration of many students. Among them was my oldest son, Ralph. Upon visiting that church, I became aware of a special style used by this pastor when he prayed: "Lord, I—*uh*—want to—thank you—*uh*—", etc.

After about four months, Ralph came home on a visit from seminary. As we prayed together, I heard: "Lord, I—*uh*—want to—thank you—*uh*—", etc. I realized that the tremendous impact of this fine man upon my son had caused him to even emulate the *"uh's"* in his prayers. Since we had a very close friendship, I felt I could talk to this pastor about the matter. The Lord spoke clearly to him about the smothering way he was training men. Soon after, he began to send two or three students at a time to spend weekends with me. He chose other pastors as well for this exposure, and with relief later reported to me, "Our guys are praying without my *"uh's."*

It's a good thing to think about people in your Cell Group or Zone who will enrich the life of your Sponsee. Arrange joint meetings between them to foster further contacts independent of your presence. There is a danger that your relationship with your Sponsee will eventually blow up if you meet your own special emotional needs by limiting his or her outside contacts and friends.

5 The Sponsor's Ministry

THE CONCEPT OF PARTNERSHIP

Establishing a relationship with your Sponsee is not to be seen as a one-way process. Although as a mentor, you have at least a *little* more experience as a Cell Group member than your Sponsee. Think of it as entering into a *partnership.* Reject any image in your mind that this is to be a top-down, parent-to-child relationship. Do not develop the friendship based on the assumption that the Sponsee has nothing to contribute. Expect to be ministered to, to be blessed, to be encouraged. God is going to work through each of you as edification takes place.

LIST YOUR EXPECTATIONS

Both of you have needs. What do each of you expect from your times together? Expectations should be clearly defined both ways. As a Sponsor, what do you hope to get in return for your investment in time and effort? What do you desire to contribute to the life of your Sponsee?

If you prayerfully think through this matter, your times together will have greater benefit for both of you.

Here is a partial list of things you might do as a Sponsor. Underline the ones which are important to you:

1. Set high expectations of performance.
2. Offer challenging ideas.
3. Help build self-confidence.
4. Encourage prayer as a lifestyle.
5. Offer friendship.
6. Confront negative behaviours and attitudes.
7. Listen to personal problems.
8. Teach by example.
9. Provide growth experiences.
10. Share significant Scriptures that have spoken to you.
11. Explain how the Cell Group functions.
12. Coach in how to share during Edification Times.
13. Be available in critical situations.
14. Offer wise counsel and words of knowledge.
15. Encourage Kingdom behaviour.
16. Awaken self-awareness.
17. Inspire to spend time in the "Listening Room."
18. Instill a love for Bible study.
19. Share critical knowledge.
20. Assist the Sponsee to become a Sponsor.
21. _____
   _____
22. _____
   _____

LIST THE SPONSEE'S EXPECTATIONS

What does your Sponsee feel is needed from the Sponsor? This should be discussed at the first session and is best done in an informal setting over a meal together.

You might say, "We'll be spending several months together as you go through the Daily Growth Guides. I want our times to meet your expectations. What do you want to accomplish as we meet? Perhaps you have some expectations for the first two or three weeks related to changes you are ready to make in your life at this time. Other expectations may develop later, but discussing those in your mind now gives us a starting point."

Some expectations, depending on how long the person has been a Christian, might include:

1. A desire to know more about how God speaks to us.
2. Interest in the other members of the Cell Group.
3. Which Bible would be a good investment to secure.
4. Help with painful problems which must be solved.
5. Assistance in understanding concepts presented in the Daily Growth Guides.
6. Bringing family members and close friends to accept Christ.
7. Getting rid of old habits that do not belong in the Kingdom of God—habits that seem to master the Sponsee.
8. Sharing exciting dreams and plans for the future, including long-range goals to be met.
9. Decisions to be made concerning career planning.
10. Relationships with husband or wife, seeking to bring Christ more into focus in the marriage.
11. Relationships with children, relatives, or siblings that may be impacted by the choice to become an active Cell Group member.
12. _____

   _____
13. _____

   _____

DEVELOP A SPONSOR-SPONSEE AGREEMENT

As you review these expectations on both sides, a vision of what God will do with you during this time will develop. Writing down in duplicate what you have shared might be a very good idea!

It is suggested that you formulate a "Sponsor-Sponsee Agreement." It need not be formally written down.

The Agreement's purpose will be to set objectives for your mutual effort. It might list the key points you have discussed about your expectations.

How will you review this Agreement? Should you both agree to a monthly evaluation? Would it help you to discern the progress you have made?

Here are a few things that might be in the agreement:

1. When and where telephone calls to each other should be made.
2. The day of the week you will consistently meet.
3. The hour you agree to promptly meet for your regular sessions.
4. That the Cell Leader may be allowed to know in confidence about personal matters discussed between the two of you.
5. Relatives or friends who might be included in social engagements you will have together.
6. The style of sharing which is preferable: for example, sharing in a private room, or meeting for a meal where you "talk things over."
7. Scripture memory will be given the highest priority, and you will hold each other accountable for scripture memorization.
8. A promise by the Sponsee that the *Daily Growth Guides* in the *Arrival Kit* will not be skipped and then crammed into one sitting for the entire week. It is agreed that for the first three weeks it will be okay for you to make random checks.

GROWTH REQUIRES THE INVESTMENT OF TIME

Bonding requires time. The more time you spend together, the stronger the relationship will become. This does not necessarily mean massive changes in your schedules or your lifestyles. Can you sit together in the Celebration service? Can you go out with your families for a meal sometime, perhaps after the Sunday Celebration or a Zone meeting? Can you share in a sport you both enjoy? Go shopping? Take the children to the zoo? Take both families on a picnic instead of doing it separately? *Anything* you do together is an investment in building a relationship that will produce precious fruit in the years ahead.

—A TRUE STORY—

She was a teenager when she began to attend a Cell Group with her parents. The Cell Leader became a second parent to her, and they enjoyed teasing each other. One time the Cell Group went to a large amusement park for a picnic, and the two of them rode the roller coaster together. They stared into each other's eyes as they hurtled downward to see who would "chicken" and blink first. She won!

The years passed, and she went away to college. Then she entered the business world in a city far away. She lost touch with a Cell Church and was bored to tears by the dryness of the churches she visited. Finally she dropped out entirely, and her prayer life was extinguished. A married man enticed her to have an affair, and she was devastated by the experience.

It was then that she called long distance: "I need you guys. I can't face my parents, even though they live near you. Can I come to stay with you for a few days and get things sorted out?" Three days later, and after many tears, she had put her life back into the hands of her Lord. The investment of time, even after all the years that had passed, provided the platform for her restoration.

MEET THE *OIKOS* OF YOUR SPONSEE

Do not ignore the *oikos* of your Sponsee. Those who have enjoyed close relationships with him or her need to know you and respect you. If you do not pay attention to this area, an unnecessary hostility can develop.

One example of this took place when a woman became the Sponsor to a lady her own age. They faithfully met weekly, and also played tennis together. One day the Sponsee's mother strongly criticized this new friendship her daughter had developed. It was only then that the Sponsor realized she had unknowingly become a "phantom person" to the mother and the other *oikos* people in her Sponsee's life. Fortunately, she was able to mend the rift before it became more serious.

Early in your relationship, drop by the home of your Sponsee and meet everyone who lives there. It is appropriate to occasionally call some of the family members and chat about their life, work, or anything that will show you have taken an interest in them. This is particularly important if there are unbelievers in the home.

IF POSSIBLE, MEET THE "PATTERN PEOPLE"

When you and your Cell Leader visited your Sponsee, you discovered the names of the two role models who have influenced him or her. (See page 10 in your Sponsee's *Journey Guide* for their names.) Are these persons alive? Is it possible for you to actually visit with them? It's a good idea to do so!

You will glean major insights which will help you in your ministry. Be affirming where these special people have made positive contributions. When they have injected negative values into the Sponsee, you may need to pray about how you will break these strongholds (see pages 76-77 in *The Arrival Kit*).

6 The Sponsor's Mission

YOUR MISSION: EDIFICATION

Let us therefore make every effort to do what leads to peace and to mutual edification. (Romans 14:19)

Since you are eager to have spiritual gifts, try to excel in gifts that build up the church. (1 Corinthians 14:12)

Jesus repeatedly taught and demonstrated that being a servant is the essence of living in the Kingdom of God. As you went through *The Arrival Kit*, you realized there is no other way to function and call ourselves *pais,* the children/servants of God.

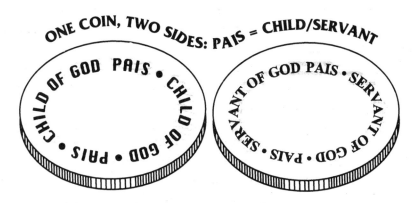

For centuries, the lifestyle of believers has been cruelly distorted by traditional church life. Perhaps you, yourself, have come from a tradition where becoming a Christian meant nothing more than attending preaching services and Bible studies. This "sitting and soaking" approach to beginning the Christian life is *never* found in the New Testament. It is a trick of Satan to neutralize believers.

In the Cell Church, you are regarded as a *pais* from the moment of your conversion, a child and a servant of God. Your entrance into the Sponsor ministry should take place within a few weeks of your conversion or your joining a Cell Group. Serving another Christian is the most important step you can take to grow in the Lord.

THE TWO NECESSARY INGREDIENTS FOR EDIFICATION

1. There must be a life situation where edification is required.
2. There must be the presence of the Holy Spirit to provide the ministry to be performed.

Beware of a "self-help" approach to being a Christian. The idea that you have to spend months or years being "grounded in the faith" before you can begin to minister to someone else is nonsense! In fact, unless you get involved in serving someone else, you are not in the proper climate to grow! Growing in the Lord is simply not possible in a self-centered life. The condition which is needed to mature as a believer is to serve another person, using the gifts of the Holy Spirit. It is only in this context that you can learn to be an edifier.

In *The Arrival Kit,* you studied about *oikos, oikonomos,* and *oikodomeo (see pages 40-53).* In your Cell Group, members are encouraged to build up or edify *(oikodomeo)* one another. If you have had no experience in edifying, your Cell Group meetings may seem awkward for you. You watch others who respond quickly to another Cell member with insights given by the Lord, and you wish *you* could do that too! You can, you should, and you will! Your times with your Sponsee will give you plenty of opportunities to learn how to build up another person. Through your Sponsor-Sponsee get-togethers, you will gradually learn how to let the Lord also flow through you in your Cell Group.

The Christ who dwells in you is the Source of all the edification you will ever do. The "Listening Room" experiences you will have as you pray over your Sponsee will reveal to you the way God speaks and empowers for ministry.

SEVEN STEPS IN EDIFICATION

1. Identify Feelings.

Small children tend to cry over things that seem to be trivial to adults. Insensitive parents often smash them by saying, "Stop that right now, or I'll spank you!" As a result, many people learned early in their lives that they should sublimate their feelings. They then become a boiling pot of angry emotions suppressed with a tight lid to keep them from erupting. The times you spend with your Sponsee may be the first opportunity he or she has to get in touch with these emotions. How do you make this happen? By prayerfully listening to the voices of your Sponsee and your Lord.

2. Discern Problems.

This can be very confusing for you as you begin your ministry. You may *know* there are problems, and your Sponsee may even make references to them. Yet, you cannot *pinpoint* the problem. What should you do?

Dr. Juanita Hart was a psychiatrist who impacted me greatly when she joined our Cell Group church in Houston in 1970. As I sat with her to observe group therapy sessions, she taught me an important principle: problems are like someone riding a carousel. The problems will rotate by you many times. If you can't sense them on the first cycle, be patient. They will reveal themselves over and over as the weeks go by. Wait until you are sure you have grasped the problem before you seek to minister to it. At the same time, listen to the voice of your Lord. Some believers, more than others, possess the gift of discernment which makes it possible for them to sense things which are hidden to others.

—A TRUE STORY—

Without any reason, the skin on my face began to peel as though I had a severe sunburn. Ointments and pills that were prescribed by physicians did not help. Looking terrible and feeling the same way, I made a trip across the

41

Eastern United States. I stopped to visit with a Cell Church pastor and his wife, having called them the day before to tell them I would be doing so.

When I arrived, they warmly greeted me. His wife said, "Ralph, as I prayed about your coming this morning the Lord told me you have a physical problem. It's your face, isn't it?" "Yes," I said. "Nothing seems to clear this up." Gently she said, "I would like to share with you what the Father gave me about this." She continued, mentioning a specific area of my past that I had suppressed long before. I readily acknowledged that her remarks were on target.

The three of us knelt together and I received deliverance from the stress related to the suppressed incident. Within ten minutes, my skin problem had totally disappeared.

3. Confront Negative Behaviours.

Too often, people do not love enough to confront others about negative behaviours. Are there harsh words, bitter comments, or a sense of gloom that should be put away? Hebrews 10:24 reminds us,

And let us consider how we may spur one another on toward love and good deeds.

Providing deliverance from old habits and detrimental manners is not done in the flesh. It is done by the Holy Spirit flowing through you. Wise speech and helping others in distress are spiritual energizings which will operate for you.

Sponsors often make their best contribution when they help their Sponsees break out of negative patterns of behaviour that occur again and again. When a person makes the same mistake repeatedly, the solution is not to give the same suggestion over and over. It would be better to look at the situations where this occurs and identify the repetitive elements so they can be changed—even if the change is painful.

For example, if your Sponsee repeatedly fails to memorize the Scripture verses for the week, there are only so many times you can say, "Try to do better next week." Warning of the consequences doesn't help either. Avoid comments like, "If you fail to memorize these verses, you won't have them in your heart when you need their guidance!" A better approach would be to discuss a mutual plan to solve the problem.

For example, a Sponsor in a college Cell Group met each day with the Sponsee to focus on the memorization of the Scripture verses. This daily coaching instilled the habit of daily memorization, and it continued on long after their schedules changed and they could no longer meet.

Is your Sponsee habitually late for every appointment with you? How do you handle it? You might ask each time, "Tell me why you were late today for our meeting?" After two or three times, you will discern a pattern of conduct that causes this character defect. After evaluating, you can discuss together a way to solve the problem.

4. Explore Options.

Frequently people are locked inside their problems, unable to see any solutions. As you take situations to your "Listening Room," additional options may be revealed to you.

—A TRUE STORY—

WEC was founded to send missionaries to unreached people. They assigned the field workers furloughing in London to be their decision-making body. Year after year, these seasoned workers would struggle over personality clashes between missionaries. Sometimes they would meet for days, trying to find ways to separate couples who could not get along with one another.

Norman Grubb wrote about one session where such a problem was being discussed. Finally, one of the men

43

said, "Let's all go to our rooms and pray about this matter. Instead of making our own decision, let's ask our Lord to tell us what would bring Him the greatest glory!" When they reassembled, one of them said, "I have a clear word on this matter." He described a healing between the couples who were fighting, and saw them working more closely than ever before.

As he shared, other men shook their heads in doubt that it could happen. One said, "Let's try it! Surely this solution would glorify God the most of all." To their delight, the action they took brought great victory to the couple. From that time onward, this policy became standard procedure for the mission directors.

There are too many times when the options considered to solve a problem do not focus on the answer to this question: *"Of all the options that might be taken in this situation, which one will bring the greatest glory to God?"* Edification of your Sponsee should always begin with that question.

5. Provide Information.

A person entering your Cell Group will have many questions which should be answered. Since you are the Sponsor, these queries will come first to you. They may be about *The Year of Equipping*, or our worship style, or how to take notes as the Pastor teaches. They may need to understand why the Cell Group occasionally skips a meeting to participate in Zone or District activities. When you cannot *provide* the information needed, be a *channel* to the source of it.

6. Help Your Sponsee Shift Paradigms

Is "paradigm" a new word for you? Imagine you have lived in a windowless room from the day you were born. You would assume that "reality" is only what has been experienced in that room. One day, a hole is cut in the wall of the room. You step through it and are astonished to see the sky, the trees, the grass, the river. You think, "This existed all the time and I never knew it! I don't want to return to the room again."

That would be called making a "paradigm shift." The whole purpose of the journey your Sponsee will take through *The Arrival Kit* is to knock out a hole in an old lifestyle and to step into the new life and light of the Kingdom of God. Many years ago, a hymn writer explained the paradigm shift with these words:

> *Heaven above is deeper blue,*
> *Earth beneath is sweeter green;*
> *Something lives in every hue*
> *That mortal eyes have never seen . . .*
> *Since I know—as now I know,*
> *That I am His, and He is mine!*

Take every occasion the Lord provides as you review *The Arrival Kit* materials to bring about changes in values.

7. Demonstrate Ministry Activity.

From the very first get-together, seek to engage your Sponsee in times of ministering to others. If your Cell Group gathers around one of the members to pray for a need, use this as a time to include your Sponsee in the intercession. Seek to go together to visit unbelievers, and to demonstrate how you go about sharing your testimony. Your Sponsee should have already prepared a testimony in your *Journey Guide* visit. Don't let this written witness fade away; create opportunities for personal witnessing. Later on, you will be going through *Touching Hearts Guidebook* together, but you need no special training to visit with *oikos* members and to share your faith as the Lord opens the way.

—A TRUE STORY—

George was working for an aircraft company when we launched the first Cell Group in his area. As I sponsored him, it became apparent that he had never, in his entire

Christian life, observed another Christian sharing his faith. I chose to schedule one of our get-togethers to visit a man George worked with every day. This man was a retired navy officer who used vulgar language and had a critical spirit. However, he had enjoyed sharing lunch breaks with George and had asked him to loan him a certain book.

Using the dropping off of the book as an excuse, we went to see this man. As George listened, I steered the conversation to allow me to share my personal testimony. Although the man's reaction was not positive, we both knew something had stirred deep inside him. When we left, he walked us all the way to my parked car and talked until we drove away. As we did so, George gushed a great sob and said, "Ralph! That man is lost!" "Yes," I said. "Now that the Lord has helped you realize that, we can begin to pray earnestly for his salvation."

Similar visits made by you and your Sponsee will open the way to reveal the need of the lost, and to create a desire to be involved in reaching others.

7 Your Weekly Meetings

The key ingredient in your ministry to your Sponsee is simply *spending time together*. The sessions do not need to be rigidly structured using the same pattern every time. Be creative in deciding what you can do collectively. Formal and fun times are both necessary. Both of you should have the freedom to suggest what would be appropriate for the next session's agenda. The important thing is the continual transmitting of yourself as a true friend. As the weeks pass, the pattern of your meetings will change as skills develop and ministry to others takes place.

BEGIN BY TRAINING IN BASIC SKILLS

A baby's first stage of development is the acquiring of *motor skills*. Holding a bottle, rolling over, crawling and walking, are necessary abilities to be developed. In the spiritual "baby stage," learning to pray, to find Scripture passages, and to share one's faith with others should be your focus.

Acquiring *concepts* comes later. To illustrate this, the next time you talk to a two-year old, ask: "What is a chair?" The child will say, "To sit on," not "an object with four legs and a seat and a back panel." The child has not yet developed the ability to think *conceptually*.

In your first few sessions, focus on what to do, rather than on ideas. Is that not what Jesus did? He said, "Men, let's go to the mountain to spend the night in prayer." He did not bother to explain to them *how* to pray at that stage. Later, they came to Him and asked, "*Lord, teach us to pray, just as John taught his disciples*" (Luke 11:1).

Why did they have to ask Him to teach them? Why didn't Jesus automatically do so? Because, until they had *observed* prayer, they would not know how to actually *do* it. The principle of "show and *then* tell" is very helpful in the first few stages of your Sponsor-Sponsee meetings. In Jesus' example, demonstration always preceded content.

Consider the impact you will make by simply bringing your own well-marked copy of *The Arrival Kit* to your first session! It will say, "I have done what you will do."

And, as you display your own well used TOUCHLink Scripture memory pack, you reveal that you are already doing what you will be helping the Sponsee to do.

TOUCHLink

"To prepare God's people for works of service"

When you pray, you will be revealing the depth of your own prayer life. As you transparently share about your own journey, you will be demonstrating that the Christian does not put on a front and hide conditions that need to be shared.

And . . . keep reminding yourself that you are only an instrument and not a source of grace! Know that the Holy Spirit will unleash and bless your relationship. Never put on an act.

THE PLACE OF THE SCRIPTURE IN YOUR RELATIONSHIP

In Deuteronomy 6:5-9, instructions were given to a Jewish father for serving as a Sponsor to his children. They were to memorize the *shimei*, the law of God. Memorization was the first step to grasping the concepts of the law of God. No child would fully grasp the implications of the long passages of Scripture which he had committed to memory. Nevertheless, internalizing the words was the first step in the process of understanding them.

Bear in mind as you read the Scripture that follows that *Moses received these instructions from God Himself:*

Love the LORD your God with all your heart and with all your soul and with all your strength. These commandments that I give you today are to be upon your hearts. Impress them on your children. Talk about them when you sit at home and when you walk along the road, when you lie down and when you get up. Tie them as symbols on your hands and bind them on your foreheads. Write them on the doorframes of your houses and on your gates.

Concentrate on Scripture memorization and the study of the many Scripture passages in *The Arrival Kit.* Instill the habit of having a daily time with the Lord by stressing the importance of doing the *Daily Growth Guides* consistently, and not cramming them into one sitting. (This is very, very important!)

THREE LEVELS YOU WILL PASS THROUGH

The initial level will focus on a *Journey Inward.* You will first journey into your own lives, peeling off layers of self-defense as you earn the right to know each other's heart. As you do so, strongholds will be revealed.

The awareness that these strongholds must be dealt with will lead to the second level, *Ministry Times.* Past pains that now causes present sufferings must be dealt with. *The Arrival Kit* has been so designed that strongholds will be presented to the Sponsee in the *Daily Growth Guides.* It will automatically lead you into this level. Your prayer times may be accompanied by tears and then rejoicing as deliverance is experienced.

The third level will involve *Value Shifts* made by the Sponsee. A love for reading the scripture, for time spent in the "Listening Room," and for participating in the Edification Times in your Cell Group will make this value shift obvious.

Each of these levels will cause you to adjust the format of your weekly meeting. Do what comes naturally!

49

PRE-PLANNING FOR YOUR WEEKLY MEETING

When I taught in a seminary, every student was required to set aside *two hours* of preparation time outside the classroom for every *one hour* spent with the professor. Since you're not in a seminary, would you compromise on a recommendation that you should spend *one* hour of preparation for every weekly meeting? Here are suggestions for this preparation:

1. Pray for your Sponsee.

This hour need not be a formal 60-minute period. You should pray daily for your Sponsee. That could involve 15 minutes of the recommended hour, scattered through the week. You may include this intercession as a part of your "Listening Room" time.

2. Write down your plans.

Next, write down your plans for the meeting. Do so a day in advance to let your thoughts "stew" in the kettle of your mind. Meditating on what you want to cover gives the Holy Spirit time to speak to your heart about the matter. Have a sense that He is your Guide as you plan the session.

3. Carefully read the Weekly Sponsor's Guides.

Your pre-planning should always include a review of the Sponsor's instructions provided for you in both the *New Believers Station* and *The Arrival Kit*. Follow these suggestions as guidelines, but don't be a slave to them. They are a starting point for you, to help you cover the materials adequately.

If you digress too far from the material the Sponsee has been studying all week, you will trigger inner frustration. Do not cause him or her to think, "I spent time every day this week going through the Daily Growth Guides—and now my Sponsor doesn't seem to care about our discussing what I have been learning!" Stay on track. If you have other areas you want to cover, do it *in addition to,* and not *in place of,* the review of the materials.

4.   Keep a record of your weekly meetings.

Record all details after each session so you don't forget them. There is a form provided for this purpose in Chapter 11 (see page 72).

—A TRUE STORY—

Anthony wasn't a very organized person. He often misplaced his briefcase and his desk looked like an explosion of paper. He was preparing to be a Sponsor for the first time.

He was required to take a medical exam for a new job. When he went to see his doctor, the nurse presented a file to the physician with his name on it. "I see you had a spot on your lung two years ago, Anthony," said the doctor. "Let's check that out." As the doctor tapped his chest, Anthony said, "I had forgotten about that spot! Glad you remembered it." The doctor replied, "I see several hundred people a month. If I didn't keep accurate records, some of them would be in their coffins today!"

It only takes a few moments for you to jot down the results of each session. The things you write should be kept as confidential as your personal diary. They will be extremely helpful to you in your prayer times. As the weeks go by, reviewing your records will reveal behaviour patterns you would have otherwise missed.

If you are like Anthony—not a very organized person—you may be inclined to skip this five-minute record-keeping task after each meeting. However, you need to do this more than the person who is always neat and precise. If you will be faithful in doing so, you will find that other areas of your life will be strengthened.

5.   A suggested time frame.

Here's a time frame that many Sponsors have used for the weekly sessions. Vary it as you wish, but at least it's a starting place for you. (There is a form on page 69 to help you do this.)

51

MINUTES	ACTIVITY
15	Sharing.
5	Review of Scripture memory verses.
20	Discussion of *New Believers Station* or *The Arrival Kit* materials.
10	Application of truths learned.
10	Intercession for one another and for unsaved friends.

Your first cycle of helping someone as a Sponsor will be a time of great growth for you. The second time you do so, the experience from the first time will give you greater confidence. It is through this process that you will be developing the ministry skills that will prepare you for a time when you, yourself, will become a Cell Leader. Keep reminding yourself that true spiritual maturity cannot develop until you are engaged in fulfilling this definition of a Sponsor:

One who binds himself to answer for another; one who is responsible for another's default.

8 Principles to Remember

There are certain principles you need to follow when you become a Sponsor and are responsible for another person spiritually. These come from a biblical perspective, and from many trial-and-error experiences by those who have preceded you in this ministry.

REMEMBER THE "HULA HOOP" PRINCIPLE

Hula hoops are large round, thin rings that kids swing around their bodies, using their hips as the energy to keep them rotating. There has to be enough space for the hoop to twirl around the body.

The "hula hoop principle" suggests you leave some "space" between you and your Sponsee. It stresses the importance of not controlling your Sponsee too closely.

Another way of illustrating this principle comes from Australia. Those who live in the Outback may have their nearest neighbor "drop in" from a journey of 1,000 kilometers. A man who studied these people discovered those who live in the bush need more physical space between themselves and others while holding a conversation. Those who are brought up in a city and who rub shoulders daily on buses actually require less personal space than bush people! Someone in Brisbane tested out the principle by not keeping a reasonable distance from Outbackers. He told me that without exception they would take a step backward.

Every person needs a "hula hoop" space to feel comfortable around others. You will have to decide how close you can get, both spiritually and emotionally, to the person you are working with. Trial and error is needed, but as you test it, it is better to stay further away than to press in too close.

While living in the bush can cause a person to need more physical space, those who seem to need the most emotional space are those who have been mauled in the past. I am thinking of a man who was given away by his parents to a relative at birth because they didn't want to raise another child. This cruel rejection impacted him deeply, and he finds it hard to draw close to others. Rejection had become a stronghold that causes him to live in fear.

Be sensitive to the openness of your Sponsee. Don't try to get too close too fast. Trust will develop as it becomes obvious you are not going to apply "smother love" in the relationship.

DON'T SOLVE THE SPONSEE'S PROBLEMS

If you take over problems from the Sponsee, you will do great harm. Often it seems easier to solve them using your own resources rather than those available to the Sponsee. Contributing your time, your insights and your love is what is truly needed.

—A TRUE STORY—

Elaine came to our Cell Group from a distant city. She finally shared with us that she had run up debts totalling thousands of dollars through her charge cards. She shared this with many tears. At the close of the meeting, Cliff came up to me and said, "Ralph, I could easily pay off her debts, and we could give her a new start. What do you think?" I replied, "I think we would create great problems for her if she gets that sort of help!" Instead, we went to her apartment and made her list all the debts she had accumulated. We said, "Elaine, you incurred these debts, and you are going to have to pay them yourself. To do that, you must take two jobs and work 16 hours a day. We will help you get in touch with your creditors. You give them a pay-back schedule and ask their cooperation."

"I can't do it!" she replied. "I won't have any time to cook or wash or even come to Cell Meeting." "We have thought about that," we said. "The women in our Cell will clean your apartment, wash your clothes, and leave cooked food in your refrigerator. We will not abandon you—but you must learn to be accountable for your finances, and we will not give you money."

For one year, we drove past the store where she worked at night until midnight. We would stop and pray with her. It was a very difficult year for her, but at the end of it we had a party to celebrate her becoming debt free.

The desire to "do it myself" is critical to growth. Honor the Sponsee's specialness by offering to help *find* solutions without *becoming* the solution. People seldom want to be told what they should do or how to do it, but they appreciate an idea or a bit of information offered in a neutral way.

NEVER, EVER GIVE OR LOAN MONEY DIRECTLY TO THE SPONSEE

There were no needy persons among them. For from time to time those who owned lands or houses sold them, brought the money from the sales and put it at the apostles' feet, and it was distributed to anyone as he had need. (Acts 4:34-35)

Financial aid given to Cell Group members first went through the hands of the apostles. There is an important reason for observing this principle. When one member of a Cell Group makes direct contributions, a sense of obligation remains in the mind of the receiver which often destroys the relationship. *It is never a good idea to loan money or give funds directly to your Sponsee!* If the Lord tells you to help in some way, discuss the matter in private with your Cell Leader and Zone Supervisor. Your giving should be done anonymously. Do not ignore this advice!

HELP THE SPONSEE
MAKE FINAL DECISIONS ALONE

You are encouraged to listen to your Sponsee's problems and spiritual battles, but do not try to make final decisions for him or her. That is the responsibility of the Sponsee. Following your instructions on these problems lessens the Sponsee's ownership. It becomes a way to avoid responsibility for what happens. You *never* want to hear these words: *"Well, I did what you told me to do, and now look at the mess I am in. I never should have taken your advice!"* Let the Sponsee use his or her own style to adapt your help to the situation. This enables the Sponsee to wrestle with the details, perhaps try different approaches, and discover his or her inner strengths and the leadership of the Holy Spirit.

The problem explained by your Sponsee usually contains both a *fact* and a *feeling.* A comment like, *"I have a problem with my employer that just won't let go of me!"* is a factual statement of what is perceived, but it also reveals the *feelings* that are present. They might include anger, fear, a desire for revenge, etc. Seek to draw out both the facts and the feelings, and minister in both areas. Saying, *"Oh, my! Let's just ask the Lord to help you."* may communicate you are not willing to struggle with the Sponsee about the issue.

It is quite possible that the Sponsee will decide to do something his or her own way and not choose to do what you have suggested. This does not mean that your ministry has been ineffective. An efficient Sponsor lets go, or more importantly, doesn't take charge in the beginning, of the Sponsee's decision-making. A helping relationship is a liberating relationship.

REMIND THE SPONSEE THAT
WALKING IN VICTORY IS A CHOICE

The Sponsor must not make choices for the Sponsee, but through prayer and counsel, point out that walking in victory is a choice! In *The Arrival Kit,* Romans 8:38-39 is deliberately inserted to be memorized in Week 2, so you can use it to stress that we can walk in victory in spite of circumstances. Share your own testimony about circumstances when you chose happiness instead of gloom, trusting in Christ to intercede, and how peace came to your heart.

EXPLAIN THAT "YOU NEVER FAIL UNTIL YOU QUIT."

We seldom mention the word *"perseverance"* in everyday conversation, but it is very important to practice it! Scriptures refer many times to the importance of not quitting before we reach the finish mark. The writer of Hebrews uses the analogy of a runner in a race to speak of this:

> *Therefore, since we are surrounded by such a great cloud of witnesses, let us throw off everything that hinders and the sin that so easily entangles, and let us run with perseverance the race marked out for us. Let us fix our eyes on Jesus, the author and perfecter of our faith, who for the joy set before him endured the cross, scorning its shame, and sat down at the right hand of the throne of God. (Hebrews 12:1-2)*

James 5:11 refers to Job's perseverance during the terrible calamities that befell him. We are reminded of what the Lord finally brought about in his situation. In 1:3-4, James wrote:

> *. . . you know that the testing of your faith develops perseverance. Perseverance must finish its work so that you may be mature and complete, not lacking anything.*

Spiritual growth involves learning to practice the presence of God in the valleys of our lives. God has given all the resources we need to stand firm.

9 Dealing With Problem Areas

If any of you lacks wisdom, he should ask God, who gives generously to all without finding fault, and it will be given to him. (James 1:5)

As a level of deep trust is reached, problem areas in the life of your Sponsee will be shared. It is an honor to be trusted with this information. It will indicate that confidence and respect for you has been created. These moments are special times for you. They provide an opportunity for the spiritual gift of discernment, or the gift of wise speech, to be manifested through you. This energizing of the Holy Spirit must be the basis for your discussion of the Sponsee's problem:

Now to each one the manifestation of the Spirit is given for the common good. To one there is given through the Spirit the message of wisdom, to another the message of knowledge by means of the same Spirit . . . (1 Corinthians 12:7-8)

The way you go about helping your Sponsee will model the way a Christian can bring the leadership of the Holy Spirit into a problem. Therefore, it is important that you *minister* to the problem and *not just give good advice*. In fact, you should avoid giving *any* advice at all, as we shall see. Instead the Holy Spirit provides wisdom and knowledge that will reveal to the Sponsee that your discussion is different than a visit made to a secular counselor.

Thoughtfully read this scripture:

But the wisdom that comes from heaven is first of all pure; then peace-loving, considerate, submissive, full of mercy and good fruit, impartial and sincere. (James 3:17)

Please underline the *eight characteristics* of *"the wisdom that comes from heaven"* in the above verse. Meditate on them. You will know the Holy Spirit is working through you when what you do and say are marked by these characteristics.

Enter the discussion of a problem area with a Spirit-filled mind! Pray silently or verbally as the problem is shared. Make it evident to the Sponsee that your discussion is a *three-way* sharing, and the two of you must not come to your own conclusions.

Imagine Paul observing the two of you as you are discussing a problem. He might turn to someone like Timothy or Luke standing nearby and say,

> *[May they] . . . be encouraged in heart and united in love, so that they may have the full riches of complete understanding, in order that they may know the mystery of God, namely, Christ, in whom are hidden all the treasures of wisdom and knowledge. I tell you this so that no one may deceive you by fine-sounding arguments. (Colossians 2:2-4)*

To the two of you he would give this loving advice, so beautifully demonstrated in all his writings:

> *I keep asking that the God of our Lord Jesus Christ, the glorious Father, may give you the Spirit of wisdom and revelation, so that you may know him better. (Ephesians 1:17)*

> *Let the word of Christ dwell in you richly as you teach and admonish one another with all wisdom, and as you sing psalms, hymns and spiritual songs with gratitude in your hearts to God. (Colossians 3:16)*

1. The first step is to listen, listen, *listen!*

Listen to your Sponsee and listen to your Lord at the same time. Experience operating under the direction of the Holy Spirit. When you manifest true spiritual gifts, you are a channel between the *Source* and the *situation*. One of the great advantages of your being a Sponsor is that you are provided with situations where you can become a channel of God's grace to the Sponsee. Listen both ways.

As a problem is shared, it will take some discussion before the full details will be known to you. The Sponsee knows more about the problem than you do, and may feel that some details cannot be shared. They may be omitted intentionally because they are self-incriminating, or simply because they may be considered irrelevant. Listen and ask questions until you fully understand the details of the problem.

As you listen, reflect on the emotions being expressed. Confirm that you understand the depth of the pain involved. Paraphrase what you are hearing by saying something like, "So you felt great resentment swelling up inside you?" Ask, "Am I understanding the situation correctly?"

In this listening stage, offer your thoughts only when they are asked for through a question like, "What do you think I should do?" A good way to answer such a direct plea for a solution would be to say, "What is the Lord saying to you about what to do?" You might even pause for a moment of prayer asking Him to provide wisdom. Without giving your conclusions, help your Sponsee to arrive at the solution.

Should you prematurely offer a solution and then ask, "Why don't you solve the problem this way?" you may get an immediate reply which begins with *"Yes, but—"* Such a reply should be seen as a a red flag. Stop your advice-giving! This response by the Sponsee shows you are seen as presumptuous and even a little arrogant, assuming you know more about the Sponsee's personal problems than the Sponsee does. The final choices must be made without pressure from you. Avoid insisting he or she agree to a specific plan you feel is correct.

2. In place of *advice*, offer *insights*.

People don't want advice. You will be respected for your experience and insights, not your advice. Your insights may be the most crucial assistance you can offer. The spiritual gift of discernment must operate in your life. If you cannot sense the leadership of the Holy Spirit as you complete the initial discussion of the problem, do not proceed. It is most appropriate to stop and pray, and to say, "Let's come back to this after we both have had time to present it to the Lord in our "Listening Rooms." On page 44, this principle was used by WEC to find the solutions to problems in the Mission:

> "Instead of making our own decision, let's ask our Lord to tell us what would bring Him the greatest glory!"

Using a problem to find God's plan is a vital part of Kingdom life. After you experience a few cycles of problem-solving using this principle, you will always avoid offering human solutions to difficulties.

3. The unhappy results of offering advice:
    The Sponsee cries, "Help! Tell me what to do!"
    The Sponsor gives advice to solve the problem. Without being aware of what is happening, this message is sent: "Sponsee, you are inadequate and I must rescue you!"

Obviously, this is not the message that was intended, but nearly always it is the one transmitted. It sours the relationship!

4. Don't get caught in this trap:
    The Sponsor says: "You ought to . . . ," "You need to . . ."
    The Sponsee responds, "Yes, but . . ." (The Advice is rejected.)
    The Sponsor tries again, offering new advice . . .
    The Sponsee responds to each new idea with, "Yes, but . . ."

The Sponsor gets disgusted and thinks, "You don't really want to solve this problem!" Because it would be rude to verbalize such a thought, a lame excuse is made for dropping the subject. The Sponsee now feels new rejection in addition to still suffering from the old problem.
    The relationship between the Sponsor and the Sponsee sours. The Sponsee now feels the problem is too big to be solved by

anyone. Excuses are made for not being available for the next session with the Sponsor.

5. The value of offering information.

When the Sponsor offers information, the responsibility for problem-solving must remain with the Sponsee. The information can come from scripture, from personal experience, or from something that has been published. (For example, the book *Happiness is a Choice* is excellent to give to someone who always sees the dark side of life.)

The Sponsor will provide much help by asking questions that focus on elements of the situation that seem to be repeated over and over again. An example of this would be a discussion of the times when discouragement strongly attacks. What were the circumstances that triggered the discouragement? Often, situations that seem different actually have the same conditions within them that cause the "blues" to surface.

List all possible alternatives as you pray and discuss the problem. As the Lord gives you insights, do not say, "I have your only solution . . ." This leaves little room for the Sponsee to personally experience the Lord speaking directly about the matter.

Instead, you can expect the Lord to guide the Sponsee to discover His leadership. Use words like these: "Have you considered . . . ?" Give the Holy Spirit time to *work in* what is to be *worked out.*

6. Avoid being critical.

Being judgmental will not help. It generates defensiveness in the Sponsee. Remember that two of the most powerful motivations in our lives are *survival* and *security.* When a person is not trusting the Lord for these two things, many wrong judgments will be made.

Nagging never changes people. We have all personally experienced nagging behavior and disliked it. In spite of that, we often use it anyway. Seek to avoid this way of talking.

7. Focus on the gap: discovering the will of God.

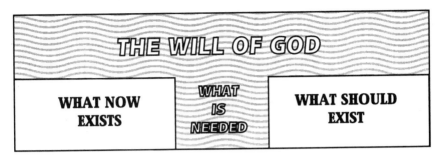

The focus is on the gap—*what is needed* is the will of God in the midst of the problem.

8. Avoid rescuing your Sponsee from his or her own folly.

Genuine victims are people who have been hurt through no fault of their own. They need support, love, and affirmation. Their inner pain needs to be removed through ministry times, and the anger and resentment need to be dissipated.

However, a different situation exists where sin has been committed and its consequences have to be faced. It is not possible to rescue people from their own folly.

An example of this was a mother who came to me greatly worried because her 23-year-old son was on drugs. She wanted him to stop, and was greatly troubled by his habit. When I asked where he got the money to buy drugs, she admitted she gave it to him to keep him from stealing! The total folly of her actions was not evident to her. She was slowly using up her life savings to support his habit. She could not be rescued through any amount of counseling!

A different example is the true story of a well-known doctor who molested boys who came to him for treatment. When he was finally caught, he rushed to see his pastor, asking him to intercede with the police. The pastor said, "I will not stop the due process of law because of your actions. You must face the consequences of your sin. But I will walk through this terrible ordeal with you and be your friend." The man went to prison, lost his practice, and disgraced his family. Through his entire ordeal, the pastor remained constant in his visitation to the man and in his ministry to the family.

A third example is a cell member who confided in a Sponsor that for years she had borrowed money from loan sharks. The plea for Cell Group members to make interest-free loans to help appease her creditors, who were threatening her, was flatly rejected. Such an approach would have only encouraged this person to continue to manipulate money matters in the future.

If you find yourself in situations where a person does not want to be rescued from wilful sinning, you will need help from your Cell Leader or a pastor. Be sure to get permission from the Sponsee to break your confidentiality before you share the problem. If this permission will not be granted, explain that you can do nothing further to help, except pray and listen.

Scripture makes it plain that what we sow, we reap. There is no antidote to reaping the results of sin and disobedience. However, your personal relationship must always be one of being "called alongside to help." The knowledge shared with you is not proper cause for displaying rejection. If you develop negative feelings about your relationship, this is a warning that something is wrong in your own life. While you may be bound not to share the details of the situation, it will be important for you to talk and pray through with a trusted friend (your own Sponsor?) the reason you are unable to properly minister to your Sponsee.

9. Deal honestly with repeating negative behavior.

Sometimes the Sponsee will struggle with a habit or an attitude that recurs repeatedly. It may be an addiction to something, a sexual gratification, angry outbursts of temper, etc. Often the person cannot locate the source of the problem.

For example, a young mother would go on a drinking binge about once a month, disappearing for two or three days. Her husband and children went through many traumas as she dropped out of their lives. After becoming a Christian, it didn't stop. The Sponsee discovered that as a child she had been repeatedly molested by her father, that she had a terrible image of herself, and pressures triggered the escapades.

After the problem was identified, the next step was to discover the pattern of events that triggered it. The Sponsee agreed to call the Sponsor whenever the pressure began to grow. Through these discussions, it was discovered that she had been watching a violent movie on television that often included rape. Declaring these movies off limits helped, but it was not the final solution. Many hours of ministry were required, and she was delivered from several strongholds. Eventually she felt a complete release from her malady.

You cannot rescue your Sponsee. If a conduct is repetitive, be prepared to share in the problem until it is solved. Seek help from those in the Cell Church structure as needed. Know that the Lord placed you in this person's life to grow you as well as to help someone else.

10. How to handle the repeatedly-stated problem.

A Cell Group may have a person who shares a problem over and over and over—without any apparent victory—until the group could scream! This person is usually an overtalker who is insensitive to the way the group is being dominated by prolonged harping on the problem. What should be done to help such persons?

Invariably, they will be seen as "stuck" in their problem. They are no longer trying to solve it. They just cry over it. Any attempt to suggest solutions will be rejected. In fact, they don't want to solve the problem. Without anything else about themselves to give them worth, they find their significance in talking about their problem.

In most cases, the Cell Group members feel they do not have the authority to confront the situation. It can drag on until the entire group gets exhausted. I have observed a group then pounce on some passing comment made by this person and strongly attack it as a way of expressing their resentment against the overtalker.

Ephesians 4:15 reminds us we are to *"speak the truth in love."* If your Cell Leader assigns you to work with such a person, don't cringe! Instead, thank the Lord for the experience you are about to have.

In the first session the "old tape" is replayed by the Sponsee, you need to speak the truth in love. "Susan, I wonder if you are aware of how many times you have already repeated that to me? Would you like to talk about why you continually dwell on these details?" The response will probably be surprise and confusion; for a long time, no one has had the courage to talk like that to her. If it is not appropriate to say anything more at that time, let it drop. Perhaps that's all the Lord wants the person to hear at the start.

When the tape is next played, seek to identify the problem. You are staring directly into a stronghold in this life! Satan has been robbing the Sponsee of peace and joy. You are talking to a victim of his evil work. In your "Listening Room," seek the word of the Lord. You will gradually know how to help release your Sponsee from this bondage. Often it will require others to assist you. Your fellow Cell Group members may be the ones you will consult, or perhaps a pastor.

It is simply not God's will for such a person to be placed in our midst and for the Cell Group and the Sponsor to be afraid to tackle the problem. It is important to *speak the truth in love!"*

11. Use special tools to help in ministering to the Sponsee.

One Sponsor recently said to me, "I often use a case history, or an illustration, to launch the time of sharing with my Sponsee. It is neutral, and naturally leads into applications in our own lives."

That's a great idea! There are many tools you can use to help your Sponsee. They include audio or video cassette tapes, recorded sermons by your Pastor, books or chapters from books, news clippings, special Scripture passages, your personal experiences. There are many ways you can bring in outside tools to help you. Be alert to them.

10 Preparing Your Sponsee to Sponsor

As mentioned in the Introduction (page 5), being a Sponsor does not last indefinitely. After three or four months, you and your Sponsee will become partners as you move out together to share your faith with unbelievers. You will share in the *Touching Hearts Guidebook* training. Use the term *"Partners"* to describe your relationship.

At the same time, you will want to help your Sponsee become a Sponsor of another person coming into your Cell Group. Your relationship as *Partners* will involve you in visits to Type "A" unbelievers and the sharing of the John 3:16 diagram. As you travel to and from these engagements, focus on the ministry of your Sponsee as a Sponsor. In addition, telephone calls should connect you together as needed when questions arise.

Simply be there for your Sponsee. The knowledge that you are a backup if a problem is encountered will be reassuring.

HOW TO LAUNCH YOUR SPONSEE

After your last session together, arrange a visit between the Sponsee and your Cell Leader for the signing of the VERIFICATION OF COMPLETION form on page 144 of *The Arrival Kit*. Prior to this, discuss with the Sponsee the importance of following in your footsteps and sponsoring a new Cell Group member. As you meet with the Cell Leader, make your personal recommendation that your Sponsee be assigned to an incoming Cell Group member. Let the Cell Leader arrange for the Sponsee to be taken along when the next Journey Guide visit is made. Then, remain in the background to help as you are needed. Be a "coach" whenever necessary. You are now *partners* in ministry!

11 Useful Forms

Photocopy these forms
for use in a notebook.

WEEKLY MEETING PLANNING SHEET

Week _____ Date of Meeting _____ Place _____

MINUTES	ACTIVITY
_____	Sharing: _____
_____	**Review of Scripture Memory Verses**
_____	**Discussion of Materials:**

New Believers Station, pages ___ to ___
The Arrival Kit, pages ___ to ___
Additional items I want to bring along:

_____
_____

_____ Application of truths I want to stress:

_____
_____

_____ Intercession:

_____
_____

Remarks:

REFLECTIONS FROM OUR MEETING

Name of Sponsee:_____

Date of meeting: _____ Length of time: _____

Insights Gained:

_____

_____

_____

_____

_____

Areas for Intercessory Prayer:

_____

_____

_____

_____

Additional thoughts:

_____

_____

_____

_____

_____

SCHEDULED DATES FOR COMPLETION OF
THE "YEAR OF EQUIPPING"

Name of Sponsee: _____

The "Year of Equipping"

Date to begin: _____   Date to complete: _____

New Believer's Station

Date to begin: _____   Date to complete: _____

The Arrival Kit

Date to begin: _____   Date to complete: _____

Touching Hearts Guidebook

Date to begin: _____   Date to complete: _____

Interest Groups

Date to begin: _____   Date to complete: _____

Cover the Bible, First Quarter

Date to begin: _____   Date to complete: _____

Cover the Bible, Second Quarter

Date to begin: _____   Date to complete: _____

Cover the Bible, Third Quarter

Date to begin: _____   Date to complete: _____

Cover the Bible, Fourth Quarter

Date to begin: _____   Date to complete: _____

Projected date for Sponsee to receive certificate of graduation from the "Year of Equipping:"_____

Projected date for me to receive certificate of graduation from the "Year of Equipping:"_____

REPORT OF WEEKLY MEETINGS

(Share this with your Cell Leader after the last session.)

Date of Meeting: Materials Used or Discussed:

1. _____   _____
2. _____   _____
3. _____   _____
4. _____   _____
5. _____   _____
6. _____   _____
7. _____   _____
8. _____   _____
9. _____   _____
10. _____   _____
11. _____   _____
12. _____   _____
13. _____   _____
14. _____   _____
15. _____   _____
16. _____   _____
17. _____   _____